HOW DID WE FIND OUT
ABOUT GERMS?

HOW DID WE FIND OUT...SERIES

Each of the books in this series on the history of science emphasizes the process of discovery.

"How Did We Find Out" Books by
Isaac Asimov

HOW DID WE FIND OUT THE EARTH IS ROUND?

HOW DID WE FIND OUT ABOUT ELECTRICITY?

HOW DID WE FIND OUT ABOUT NUMBERS?

HOW DID WE FIND OUT ABOUT DINOSAURS?

HOW DID WE FIND OUT ABOUT GERMS?

HOW DID WE FIND OUT

ABOUT GERMS?

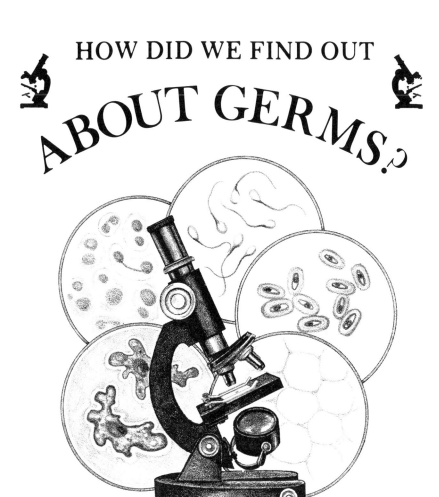

Isaac Asimov
Illustrated by David Wool

WALKER AND COMPANY
New York

First published in the United States of America in 1974 by the Walker Publishing Company, Inc.

Published simultaneously in Canada by Fitzhenry & Whiteside Limited, Toronto.

Trade ISBN: 0-8027-6165-8
Reinf. ISBN: 0-8027-6166-6
Library of Congress Catalog Card Number: 73-81402

Printed in the United States of America.

10 9 8 7 6 5 4 3 2 1

To Nick Sagan and his parents

CONTENTS

1 How Germs Were Discovered   11

2 Where Germs Come From   21

3 Disease   31

4 Germs and Disease   41

5 The Smallest Germs   55

6 Index   63

Anton van Leeuwenhoek and his microscope

1 How GERMS Were Discovered

IN THE ANCIENT LATIN language any tiny bit of life from which a much larger living thing (or "organism") can develop was called a "germen." In English, the word was shortened to "germ."

But how small can a germ—any tiny bit of life—be?

At first, the smallest bits of life people knew about were certain tiny seeds out of which plants grew. They were barely large enough to see. Could there be living bits of life too small to see? How could anyone know?

Of course, there were ways to make things seem larger. In ancient times, some people had noticed that when you looked at objects through pieces of curved glass, they appeared larger.

It was not until about 1650, though, that scientists carefully studied small things after making them appear larger by looking at them through bits of curved glass. Such bits were called "lenses" from a Latin

11

word meaning "lentil" because they were shaped like lentil seeds.

When small living things were looked at through lenses, they appeared much larger. Many details of their bodies could be seen clearly that could not be seen without lenses.

More than one lens was usually used, and they were placed at opposite ends of the metal tube so they would stay in the proper position for seeing. Such a tube was called a "microscope" (MY-kroh-SKOPE) from Greek words meaning "to see small things." Lots of tiny, living, creeping things were looked at—especially fleas. For this reason the earliest microscopes were called flea glasses.

These first microscopes were quite poor. The glass used for the lenses was not very good. It had bubbles in it and the surface of the lens was not very smooth. Anything that was enlarged by the use of such lenses looked a little fuzzy. If stronger lenses were used to enlarge it still more, everything got so fuzzy that nothing could be seen at all.

In the Netherlands, however, Anton van Leeuwenhoek (LAY-ven-hook) was doing his best to improve lenses. He was not a trained scientist since he had very little education. He owned a dry goods store and served as custodian at the city hall of his home town.

But really what he cared about was making lenses. He carefully picked out small bits of glass that had no bubbles in them at all. Then he polished them until the surface was very smooth and evenly curved.

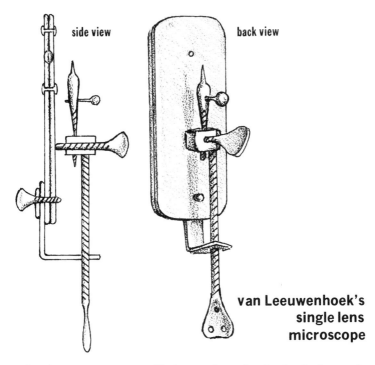

side view   back view

van Leeuwenhoek's
single lens
microscope

The lenses were small, but when he looked through them he found that the objects he looked at appeared to be enlarged up to two hundred times and still seemed sharp.

Altogether he made 419 microscopes and lenses. Making one was very slow work because of the careful way he went about it. Still, he lived to be 90 years old and he worked his whole life!

Leeuwenhoek used his excellent little lenses and microscopes to look at insects, skin, blood, hair, and anything else he could find. In 1677, he even sucked up a little drop of water from a pond and looked at it through one of his small lenses. He saw tiny little things in the water.

They were tiny, to be sure, less than a fiftieth of an inch in size, but they moved about and ate things. They were *living*, even though they were too small to see without a microscope. No man before Leeuwenhoek had ever suspected that such tiny living things existed.

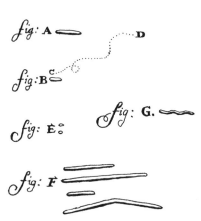

van Leeuwenhoek's figures of bacteria from the human mouth

Any living creature too small to be seen without a microscope is now called a "microorganism" (MY-kroh-AWR-gun-iz-um). Leeuwenhoek was the first man to see microorganisms. A microorganism is usually made up of a single cell which is a tiny bit of living matter surrounded by a membrane. A human being is made up of many trillions of cells.

The particular microorganisms Leeuwenhoek first saw behaved like animals in many ways. They were

14

therefore considered very tiny animals. Finally, they were named "protozoa" (PROH-toh-ZOH-uh) from Greek words meaning "earliest animals." A single one of the protozoa is called a "protozoon." But Leeuwenhoek was sure that the tiny protozoa he saw first were not the tiniest bits of life there were.

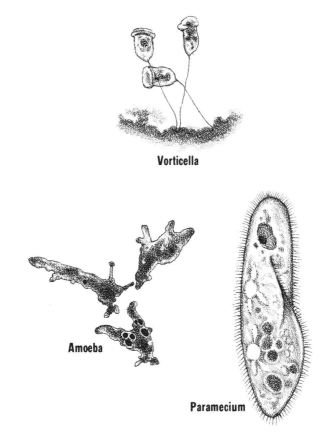

Vorticella

Amoeba

Paramecium

Different kinds of protozoa

Every time he made a better lens or microscope he could see smaller microorganisms. In 1683, he used a lens that showed him tiny things he thought might be alive. They were so tiny, however, that they looked like small dots and rods but nothing more. He just could not make a lens that was strong enough to show them clearly, and he had to give up.

Eventually, those tiny things he saw were named "bacteria" (bak-TEE-ree-uh) from a Greek word meaning "little rod." One of them is called a "bacterium." It is to these bacteria that the word

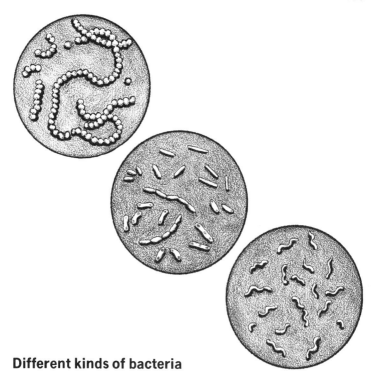

Different kinds of bacteria

"germs" is now most often applied. Scientists prefer to call them bacteria, but to most people they are germs.

Leeuwenhoek was the first person who saw germs, and for a hundred years afterward no one else could do any better.

A Danish biologist named Otto Friedrich Muller finally did manage to make them out a bit more clearly in the 1780s. He died in 1784, but a book he wrote toward the end of his life was published in 1786. He was the first scientist to try to separate bacteria into groups according to their different shapes.

He saw some that looked like tiny straight rods, for instance, and others that had a spiral shape like tiny corkscrews. He couldn't see much more than that, though.

There was a problem. No matter how clear the glass used for lenses was and no matter how carefully the lenses were shaped, what was seen in the microscope stayed a little fuzzy. It stayed fuzzy enough to make it hard to see things as small as bacteria.

Lenses bend light rays in order to make objects seem enlarged, but they do not bend all colors by the same amount. Ordinary light is a mixture of many colors, and this meant that when microscopes managed to enlarge tiny objects sharply in one color the other colors were fuzzy. For that reason, bacteria always had a colored fuzz about them. It seemed nothing could be done.

In 1830, however, an English lensmaker, Joseph Jackson Lister, combined two different kinds of glass to make lenses. Each kind bent colors a different way and the two ways cancelled each other out. In combination, the enlargement was sharp in all colors. For the first time, biologists could see bacteria really clearly.

Using these new microscopes, a German biologist, Ferdinand Julius Cohn, began to study microorganisms very carefully. He studied not only protozoa but also single-celled organisms that were plantlike in nature. They did not move about as protozoa did. They had a thick wall around them and they were green. These plant microorganisms are called "algae" (AL-jee) from a Latin word for "seaweed," because seaweed is made up of a large collection of such cells.

Cohn then went on to study bacteria, which are far smaller than either protozoa or algae. An average bacterium is only about 1/5000 of an inch across. Even so, with the new microscopes Cohn had no trouble seeing them clearly.

All through the 1860s he studied them, checking their shapes, how they lived, what kind of food they ate, how they moved about, how they multiplied by growing and then splitting in two, and so on. He classified them into different groups and subgroups and gave every division a name.

In 1872, he published a large book in three volumes about these little bacteria. He was the first one to study them as thoroughly as biologists had studied large organisms. In fact, he had established a new branch of science—a branch called "bacteriology" (bak-TEER-ee-OL-uh-jee), which means "the study of bacteria." Cohn founded the science nearly two hundred years after Leeuwenhoek had seen bacteria for the first time.

By the time Cohn published his book, though, bacteria had proved to be much more than tiny things that no one could see without a microscope. In spite of the fact that they were so tiny and invisible to ordinary eyes, they proved to be of great importance to mankind.

They became so important because biologists wondered where bacteria came from.

2 Where GERMS Come From

PEOPLE HAD BEEN WONDERING where many kinds of organisms came from. In the case of large plants and animals there was no problem. Everyone knew that animals gave birth to live young or laid eggs. Everyone knew that plants grew from seeds. They knew that each plant and animal came from other plants and animals like itself. Oak trees came from oak trees, dogs came from dogs, human beings came from human beings.

Bugs and worms, though, were something else. They seemed to come from nowhere. Some people felt that these simple little forms of life arose from dead matter. Somehow, they felt dead matter could become alive without help from the outside. This was called the theory of "spontaneous generation."

A good example of spontaneous generation was what happened to ordinary meat when it decayed. From nowhere, it seemed, little worms called maggots appeared on it. Those maggots, people said, arose from the dead meat by spontaneous generation.

In 1668, however, an Italian biologist, Francesco Redi (RAY-dee) thought he would try an experiment. After all, there were always flies around the decaying meat. Perhaps they had something to do with the maggots.

Francesco Redi and his experiment

What Redi did was to put pieces of meat at the bottom of little pots to decay. The pots were open on top, but on half of them Redi stretched pieces of gauze. Flies could get into the pots without the gauze and land on the meat. They could not get to the meat in the pots protected by the gauze.

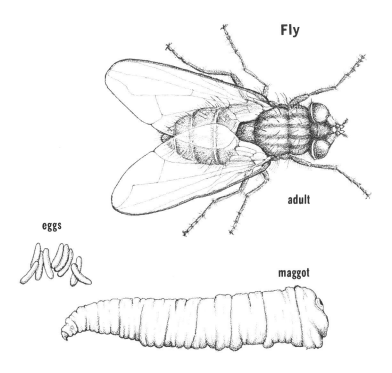

Fly

adult

eggs

maggot

All the pieces of meat decayed in the same way, but maggots developed *only* in the pieces on which flies landed. The meat that was protected by gauze never developed maggots no matter how it decayed.

Redi decided that flies laid eggs on the decaying meat and the maggots came out of those tiny eggs. They fed on the meat and eventually changed into flies in the way that caterpillars change into butterflies.

By Redi's time, microscopes existed. By using them, it was finally possible to see the eggs that flies laid in the meat. Could it be that *all* organisms, even

23

insects and worms, came out of eggs laid by other insects and worms? Could it be that living things only came from other living things and never from dead matter? Was it possible that the theory of spontaneous generation was wrong?

Biologists might have abandoned the notion of spontaneous generation, but not long after Redi's experiment Leeuwenhoek discovered microorganisms. These were living things far simpler than even the simplest insect. How about them? Perhaps microorganisms were so simple that they could form out of dead matter even though insects did not. Biologists discussed this, back and forth, for a long time.

Finally, in 1748, an English biologist, John Turberville Needham (NEED-um), tried an experiment.

He began with some mutton soup that had numerous microorganisms in it. He boiled the soup for a few minutes in order to kill those microorganisms. Then he put the boiled soup in a container which he sealed tightly.

He knew that microorganisms could not enter the flask from outside as long as the container was sealed. Any microorganisms that were to be found in the soup after he opened the seal would have to have arisen from the soup itself.

Needham let the sealed container stand a few days. Then he opened it and found that the soup was swarming with living microorganisms. Needham was certain that this proved that the theory of spontaneous generation was true, at least for microscopic organisms.

But did the experiment settle matters really? An Italian biologist, Lazzaro Spallanzani (spahl-lahn-TSAH-nee), was not at all sure. He wondered if Needham had boiled the soup long enough. Some of the microorganisms might be pretty tough and a few might survive. Needham might not have seen the few microorganisms that were still alive, and they might have multiplied while the soup was standing in the sealed container.

In 1768, then, Spallanzani began to test how long it took to kill microorganisms by boiling. He found that some were indeed hard to kill. He found that it was not safe to suppose that all the microorganisms were dead unless the soup was boiled for at least half an hour.

He then repeated Needham's experiment, but he boiled the soup for half an hour, or even more, before sealing it. He found that when this was done the soup could stand for long periods of time and never develop any microorganisms. The soup remained "sterile"—that is, without any life in it at all.

In Spallanzani's experiment, it seemed that there was no spontaneous generation after all. Even tiny microorganisms developed only from living matter, from other microorganisms like themselves.

But again not everybody was convinced. Some biologists argued that the boiling did not happen in nature. Perhaps spontaneous generation worked through some chemical in the air. Perhaps boiling destroyed that chemical, and that was why spontaneous generation did not take place after boiling. It might be that Needham's boiling had only destroyed some of the chemicals, so that spontaneous generation could still take place. Spallanzani's longer boiling, however, destroyed all of the chemical.

After all, these biologists said, if you took boiled soup and let it stand in cool, fresh air, microorganisms quickly developed. Where did they come from, if not from the soup itself with the help of the chemical that was only in the cool, fresh air?

For a hundred years, biologists argued about this back and forth. Then, in 1858, a French chemist, Louis Pasteur (pas-TEUR), tackled the problem.

In the first place, he tried to find out whether cool, fresh air might not have bacteria in it. He boiled a cotton plug in water until both the cotton and the water were completely sterile. He then pumped fresh air through the cotton plug and dipped the plug in the water. At once, microorganisms began to develop in the water. That made it seem as though there were microorganisms in the air, which got stuck by the cotton.

Could Pasteur be sure? Perhaps the microorganisms arose by spontaneous generation out of the sterile cotton or the sterile water. To test this, Pasteur filtered a quantity of air through a sterile cotton plug. Then he drew this *filtered* air through a second sterile cotton plug and placed it in the water.

This time, no microorganisms were found. They had all been removed from the air by the first plug and none developed in the sterile second plug or in the sterile water.

Louis Pasteur

In this way, Pasteur showed that there were micro-organisms floating all about us in the air, attached to dust particles. If boiled soup were exposed to the air, it was also exposed to the floating microorganisms on the dust. That was why microorganisms developed in the soup.

Then Pasteur tried to think of a way of letting fresh, cool air reach the soup without letting in any microorganisms on dust particles. If he could do that

27

and if no microorganisms developed in the soup, it meant that there was no chemical in the air that could make microorganisms grow in the soup. It would mean that microorganisms could only arise from other microorganisms and spontaneous generation would finally be disproved.

Here is what Pasteur did. He used a flask half-full of soup that was fitted with a long, narrow tube coming out of the top. This tube went straight up in the air, then curved down all the way, and then curved up again.

Pasteur boiled the soup. Steam came rushing out of the narrow tube and heated it to boiling temperature. Thus, all the microorganisms were killed both in the soup and on the glass tube.

Then Pasteur let the soup cool down. He did *not* place a stopper in the opening of the tube. He left the flask open so that the soup within was not blocked off. Cool, fresh air could drift in and out of

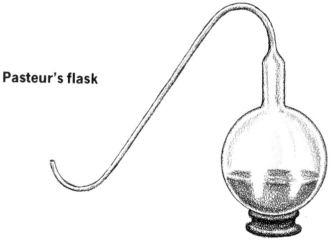

Pasteur's flask

the flask and make contact with the surface of the soup. Dust, however, could *not* enter the flask. Dust settled down at the bottom of the curve of the tube. It could not move uphill in that narrow tube.

Pasteur then let the soup stand and did not do a thing to it. Even when he let such soup stand for months, however, no microorganisms developed in the soup. The cool, fresh air and the chemicals in it might touch the soup, but as long as no dust, carrying microorganisms, touched it there was no development of microorganisms in it.

Pasteur then tried breaking off the tube of such a flask. Now dust could just fall into the soup, and overnight it was suddenly full of microorganisms.

Pasteur announced these experiments and their results in 1864. Others tried the same experiment and got the same result.

That settled it. There was no spontaneous generation. A bird came only from an egg laid by another bird; a fly came only from an egg laid by another fly; a microorganism came only from another microorganism.

This was a very important point to settle. It meant to Pasteur that, whenever he found a microorganism where it wasn't supposed to be, *it had come from somewhere else.* It could not have arisen from anything other than another microorganism.

He combined this knowledge with other work he had been doing and was able to make one of the greatest discoveries in the history of science. This discovery concerned disease.

London scene during the Black Death 1348

3 DISEASE

DISEASE IS A SUBJECT that concerns everyone. No one can ever be sure that he or she might not suddenly fall sick. A person can at any time begin to feel bad, develop a fever, or break out in a rash. Eventually, he or she might even die of a disease.

When one person falls sick, others might also. A disease can suddenly spread over a whole town or a whole region, and some diseases can be very deadly.

In the 1300s, for instance, a disease called the Black Death spread all over Europe, Asia, and Africa and killed millions of people. It was the greatest disaster in human history. One-third of all the people in Europe died.

At this time nobody in the world knew what caused disease. Some people thought demons or evil spirits took over the body. Some people thought it was bad air of some sort or another. Some people thought it was a punishment from Heaven for evil deeds.

Whatever it was, though, no one imagined the diseases could be stopped and no one knew when another Black Death might strike.

One hopeful thing about disease was that some diseases only hit a person once. If someone got measles or mumps or chickenpox and got well, then one would never get that particular disease again. He or she was "immune." His or her body had fought off the disease and had developed some kind of defense that would continue to work for many years.

One particularly dreadful disease that only struck once was smallpox. The trouble was that very often once was quite enough. Many people who got smallpox died. Many others recovered, but their faces and bodies were covered with scars left over from the terrible blisters they had had. Every once in a while, though, someone had only a light case that did not scar him or her much. When that happened, the person was just as immune afterward as if he or she had had a terrible case.

Naturally, it was much better to have a light case of smallpox than to have none at all. With a light case, you were safe for life; with none at all, you could never be sure you might not get it at any moment.

People knew that if you were near a person with smallpox you might catch it. Would it not be a good idea, then, to hang around a person with a light case? You might catch the light case and then be safe. To make sure, you might scratch your skin with a needle that had been dipped into some of the fluid in the smallpox blisters of the sick man. This was called "inoculation" (in-OK-yoo-LAY-shun).

The trouble was, though, that a person might have a light case of smallpox, yet another person catching it might get a severe case. Inoculation just was not safe.

In the 1770s, an English doctor, Edward Jenner, grew interested in a disease called cowpox. It was called that because it was found in cows and in other farm animals. The disease was something like a very mild smallpox. If a person caught cowpox from a cow, he or she would get a blister or two and that was it. People would hardly even know they were sick.

The country people where Jenner lived thought it was good luck to get cowpox because then you never got smallpox. Most doctors thought this was just a superstition, but Jenner wondered. He did notice that people who worked with farm animals a good deal hardly ever got smallpox.

After twenty years of study, Jenner decided to try a very dangerous experiment. On May 14, 1796, he found a milkmaid who had just developed cowpox. He dipped a needle into the fluid inside a blister on her hand and scratched the skin of a boy who had never had either cowpox or smallpox. The boy got cowpox and developed a blister in the place where he had been scratched.

Jenner then waited for two months to make sure the boy was completely recovered. He was now immune to cowpox, but was he also immune to *small-*

pox? Taking an enormous chance, Jenner deliberately scratched the boy with a needle that had been dipped in the fluid of a real smallpox blister. The boy did *not* catch smallpox.

Jenner tried the whole thing again two years later when he found another girl with cowpox. He again found he could make someone immune to smallpox by giving them fluid from a cowpox blister.

The medical name for cowpox is "vaccinia" (vak-SIN-ee-uh) from a Latin word for "cow." Jenner's system for giving people cowpox to save them from smallpox was therefore called "vaccination" (VAK-sih-NAY-shun). When Jenner announced his findings, vaccination was quickly adopted all over the world. Smallpox disappeared from places where vaccination was used.

Other diseases could not be defeated in the same way smallpox was. No other disease seemed to have a mild cousin that could be used to make a person immune.

Still, the whole business of vaccination made people think about the way you could transfer disease from one person to another. Maybe you could prevent people from getting sick if you stopped transferring the disease.

An Hungarian doctor named Ignaz Philipp Semmelweiss (ZEM-ul-vise) thought so. In the 1840s, he worked in a hospital where women came to have babies. Many of them died of a fever after the babies were born. Women who had their babies at home did not usually die in this way.

First vaccination by Edward Jenner

Semmelweiss wondered what made so many people die in the hospitals. In them, the mothers were treated by doctors who also worked on people who were sick or who had died. At home, the babies were delivered by women who did not deal with sick people. Could it be that the doctors were carrying disease from the sick patients to the mothers?

In 1847, Semmelweiss was placed in charge of a hospital, and he made a rule that all doctors had to wash their hands in a strong chemical solution before they came near a patient. At once, the situation improved. Hardly any mothers died in the hospital.

The doctors, however, were annoyed. They did not like to wash their hands in smelly chemicals and they did not like to be told that they were carrying a disease that killed people. Besides, they argued there was nothing on their hands so how could they be carrying a disease? They forced Semmelweiss out of his position. Then they stopped washing their hands and the mothers began to die again just as before.

But that was a problem. Could something invisible carry a disease?

Some years before he solved the problem of spontaneous generation, Louis Pasteur had begun a line of study that was to answer the question.

France's wine industry was in deep trouble at that time. Wine was turning sour when it should not have been. The wine producers were losing millions of dollars as a result.

In 1856, Pasteur was asked to investigate the problem. One of the things he did was to look at the wine under a microscope. He saw microorganisms called "yeast" in it. That was not surprising. Yeast belonged in wine. It grew in fruit juice and turned the sugar of that juice into alcohol.

When Pasteur looked at the sour wine, though, he found that some of the yeast cells present were different in shape from the usual cells. It seemed there were two kinds of yeast. The right kind turned sugar into alcohol, and the wrong kind turned the alcohol into a kind of acid.

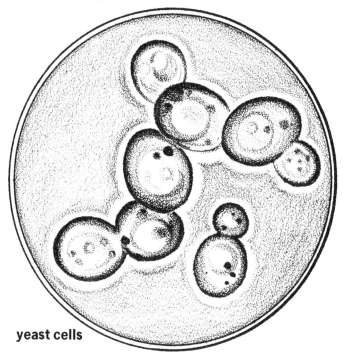

yeast cells

Yeast cells are easy to kill by gentle heating. Pasteur suggested that once the wine was formed it be gently heated. The yeast cells would be killed. The right kind of yeast had done its work and was not needed anymore. The wrong kind of yeast would be killed before it could do its acid-producing work.

The wine producers did not like to heat their wine, but they tried it. It worked. The souring of wine stopped and the wine industry was saved. Gentle heating designed to kill harmful microorganisms has been called "pasteurization" ever since. The milk Americans buy in supermarkets is always pasteurized.

Pasteur's work on wine was one of the reasons he was sure that spontaneous generation was impossible. If spontaneous generation could happen, then killing the yeast would do no good. Both kinds of yeast would be likely to arise again in the wine and it would turn sour anyway.

Pasteur could therefore move on to his great experiment on spontaneous generation quite confident that he would not grow microorganisms out of dead matter.

The work he did with wine also showed Pasteur that serious trouble could arise from the transfer of microorganisms. Suppose you put a little sour wine into wine that was not sour. The yeast that produced acid would grow in the good wine and turn it sour.

Well, then, suppose a workman was placing wine in casks and got a little on his hands. If some of the wine had the acid-producing yeast in it, the workman might have that on his hands and, without meaning to, transfer it to good wine. All the wine he worked with would turn sour.

If he washed his hands every time he began work with a new batch of wine, this might not happen.

Semmelweiss was right when he thought the doctors were carrying the disease on their hands. The reason they did not see anything was because microorganisms might have produced the disease and, of course, you can not see microorganisms on your hands.

Such thoughts may have been in Pasteur's mind at the time, but, if so, he could do nothing until he had some evidence that microorganisms were involved in disease.

4 GERMS and DISEASE

JUST ABOUT the time that Pasteur was completing his experiments that disproved the theory of spontaneous generation, a new crisis was facing France.

In the south, Frenchmen grew mulberry bushes and let silkworms feed upon their leaves. From the cocoons of those silkworms (which were really a kind of caterpillar) silk threads were drawn.

The silk industry was important to France and now, suddenly, it was being destroyed. The silkworms were falling sick and were dying, and it seemed that nothing could be done about it.

The call went out for Pasteur—no one but Pasteur. He had saved the wine industry; surely he could save the silk industry. Pasteur protested that he knew nothing about silkworms, but they begged him to come anyway.

In 1865, then, Pasteur traveled south. Once again he used his microscope. He found microorganisms present on some of the mulberry leaves but not on

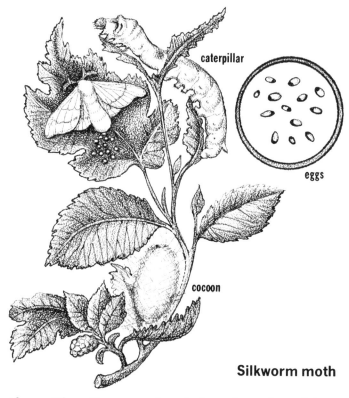

caterpillar

eggs

cocoon

Silkworm moth

others. The silkworms that fed on the infected leaves grew sick and, sure enough, those microorganisms were present in their bodies.

It was clear to Pasteur that these microorganisms were living and growing inside the silkworms. A small organism that lives and grows in a larger one is called a "parasite" (PAR-uh-site). The microorganism was parasitic on the silkworm.

What was to be done? Wine can be heated to kill yeast. That does not hurt the wine. If silkworms are heated so that the microorganisms are killed, the silkworms will die also.

Well, then, they had to die. There was no help. The only way to keep the disease from spreading was to destroy all the infected silkworms and all the infected mulberry leaves. A new beginning had to be made with healthy silkworms and healthy plants.

The people in charge followed Pasteur's advice. It worked. The silk industry was saved.

To Pasteur, it now seemed certain that disease could be caused by a microorganism. If a disease were "contagious"—that is, if it could be spread from one living thing to another—then it *must* be caused by a microorganism. Some small parasite is transferred from a sick organism to a healthy one, and then the healthy one gets sick, too.

The microorganisms can be spread through the air by coughing and sneezing. They can be spread by the hands and other parts of the body. They can be left behind in body wastes. They are too small to see and a healthy person may not know he has picked up the microorganisms until he starts getting sick himself.

Pasteur announced all this, and it is called "the germ theory of disease."

Many of the microorganisms that produce disease are bacteria, which are what we usually think of when we speak of germs. However, bacteria are not the only ones responsible. Some diseases are caused by yeasts, protozoa, or still other kinds of microorganisms.

Just because some microorganisms cause disease, however, does not mean that all of them do. Actually, only a small minority of the different kinds of microorganisms make trouble for other living creatures. The vast majority live in the soil or in water or in air and are harmless. Many of them are very useful. Some bacteria, for instance, keep the soil fertile. Others decay dead plants and animals and change them into chemicals which other plants and animals can use to grow.

Then, too, there are some diseases which are not contagious and which are not caused by microorganisms.

Still, even though there are microorganisms that do not cause disease and diseases that are not caused by microorganisms, the most important diseases of Pasteur's time *were* caused by germs. When Pasteur announced his germ theory, some doctors began to think hard about the matter.

One of these doctors was an English surgeon, Joseph Lister, the son of the man who had devised the first microscope that showed bacteria clearly. When Lister heard of Pasteur's theory, he thought of Semmelweiss. The notion of washing hands in strong chemicals might have helped cut down deaths by disease because the chemicals killed the germs on the hands.

In 1867, therefore, Lister asked doctors to wash their hands and their instruments in strong chemicals before they operated. Before that, patients often died of fevers after an operation had been carried through

Sir Joseph Lister

successfully. After the doctors started washing their hands and their instruments, however, the patients stopped dying.

Then, in 1870, France got into a war. Pasteur, who was very patriotic, tried to join the army but the French officials told him he was too old since he was almost fifty. Besides, he was more important in the laboratory, so Pasteur went to work in the hospitals where he forced the doctors to boil their instruments and steam their bandages before they touched the wounded soldiers. He saved many lives in that way.

After the war, Pasteur became interested in a disease called "anthrax" that affected cattle and sheep. It was very deadly. The very ground in which the dead animals were buried seemed to be full of the disease.

A German doctor, Robert Koch, who had worked with Cohn, the founder of bacteriology, was also interested in anthrax. He accepted the germ theory, studied the sick animals, and discovered a bacterium in them that he thought was responsible for the disease.

Koch showed that when this anthrax bacterium was outside the animal's body, it could form a thick wall about itself. It was then a "spore." A spore can live for a long time without food or water. Even boiling does not kill it. For that reason, when animals dead of anthrax were buried, the bacteria lived on in the soil as spores and healthy animals could be affected if they ate grass there.

When Pasteur heard this, he suggested that animals dead of anthrax be burned first and then buried. The burning would kill even the spores.

But Pasteur remembered Jenner's work, too. If any animal happened to survive anthrax, it never caught the disease again. If there were some mild disease similar to anthrax, the animal could be given the mild disease and would then be immune to anthrax.

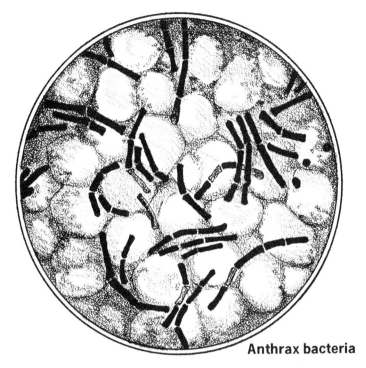

Anthrax bacteria

Unfortunately, there was no mild disease of this sort.

But now that the germ theory was understood, might a mild disease be worked out in the laboratory? Pasteur thought this might be done.

First he collected some of the bacteria from animals sick of anthrax and let them grow in special food. He then took some of the bacteria and heated them. He did not heat them enough to kill them, only enough to half-kill them. They were still alive, but they could barely grow any more.

Suppose he inoculated an animal with these "attenuated" (meaning thinned out and weakened) anthrax bacteria. The animal would not get much of a disease because the attenuated bacteria would grow so slowly. Still, the animal body, fighting off the attenuated bacteria, might develop a defense that would also work against the ordinary strong bacteria. Pasteur tried it out and the scheme seemed to work.

Anthrax experiment

In 1881, therefore, he arranged for a public test. He began with a herd of sheep and inoculated half of them with attenuated anthrax bacteria. He then waited for a period of time to let those sheep develop their defenses. Once that was done, he inoculated the entire herd with deadly, full-strength anthrax bacteria.

Within a few days every sheep that had *not* previously received the attenuated form got sick and died. Those sheep that *had* received the attenuated form just kept on eating grass. They remained healthy.

Nobody could argue about the germ theory after that, especially since it showed that doctors might now learn to control contagious diseases.

Next to Pasteur himself, Robert Koch was the most important of those who were now studying germs in connection with disease. He tried to study the bacteria he obtained from people or animals that were sick with one disease or another.

One problem was that he usually found a large number of different kinds of bacteria. It was hard to tell which ones were responsible for the disease. Instead of using soup in which to grow the germs, he began to use a kind of gelatin called "agar-agar" (AG-er-AG-er).

He placed the sterile agar-agar at the bottom of a flat dish, and when it cooled it became solid. Then he spread a small bit of bacteria-containing soup over it. There would be one bacterium in one place, another in another place, and so on. Each one would live and multiply in the agar-agar, but none of them would be able to move in the solid material. The different bacteria and their descendants stayed separate and in place. Each original bacterium would soon be

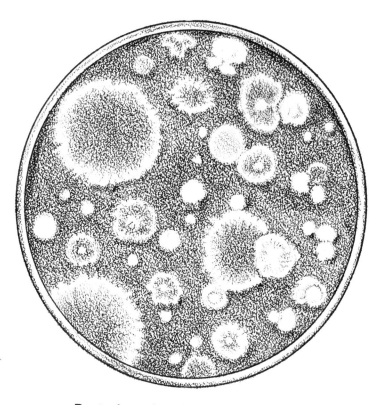

Bacteria and molds growing on agar

surrounded by a mass of its own descendants, and there would be a *colony* consisting of a single kind of bacterium and no more.

Koch could test each colony separately and then find a particular bacterium that would cause a particular disease. He discovered the bacterium that caused tuberculosis and the one that caused cholera. He even discovered the bacterium that was responsible for the Black Death.

Once the germ was known, it could be used to develop methods for preventing disease. Pasteur's method of heating the bacterium and attenuating it was one way. A German doctor, Emil Adolf von Behring (BAY-ring), who had been one of Koch's assistants, discovered another.

Behring found that the defense developed by an animal against a disease was concentrated in its blood. A bacterium liberated some poison in the blood which caused a disease. This poison was called a "toxin." What was in the blood to defend the organism against the toxin was an "antitoxin." Suppose an animal were suffering from a disease called tetanus, for instance, caused by a tetanus bacterium. Some of the animal's blood could be withdrawn. The blood could be treated in various ways to extract the antitoxin. If the antitoxin were then injected into the blood of a healthy animal, that healthy animal would gain the defenses against tetanus that the sick animal had developed. The healthy animal would not get tetanus even if the tetanus bacterium were injected into it. The healthy animal was temporarily immune.

Behring wondered if antitoxins could be developed for other diseases. At the time, one serious disease from which many children suffered was diphtheria. Behring and a friend, another German doctor, Paul Ehrlich (AIR-lik), injected the diphtheria bacterium into animals and then took out samples of blood which contained a diphtheria antitoxin.

In 1892, they had a large supply of the diphtheria antitoxin. They found that, not only did it keep healthy children from catching diphtheria, but those

51

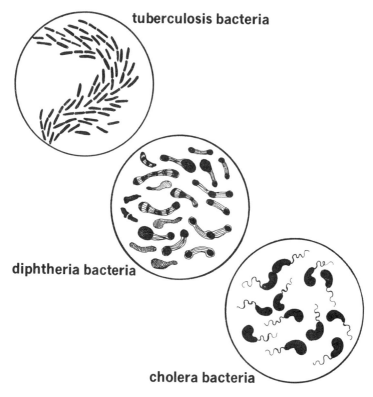

tuberculosis bacteria

diphtheria bacteria

cholera bacteria

who had already caught it were helped to get getter. People found they no longer had to fear diphtheria.

Ehrlich went on to try to attack bacteria in still another way. Perhaps there were chemicals which, if injected into a sick human being, would kill a disease germ without hurting the sick person. That would certainly help cure the disease. In 1909, he and his assistants found a chemical called "arsphenamine" (ars-FEN-uh-meen) that seemed to kill the bacterium that caused a disease known as syphilis.

Since the days of Pasteur, Koch, Behring, and Ehrlich, more antitoxins have been developed and more chemicals have been discovered which are useful against bacteria. In addition to that, people have learned to understand the reasons for good hygiene. Hands must be washed, surroundings must be kept clean, food must be fresh, water must be pure, and wastes must be disposed of carefully. That keeps germs under control.

As a result of the understanding brought to mankind by the germ theory of disease, most parts of the world no longer have to fear many contagious diseases. Now we do not have to fear that some Black Death may strike us at any moment. At least, if it does, doctors will know how to fight it.

They can even fight germs that are so small they cannot be seen in a microscope. Pasteur dealt with one disease that was caused by these super-tiny germs.

mad dog

5 The Smallest GERMS

ONE OF THE MOST FEARED diseases is called "rabies." Sometimes dogs get rabies and the sickness affects their brains. They froth at the mouth and bite everyone they can reach. They are said to be "mad dogs." If they bite human beings, those humans catch the disease after about two weeks, since it takes that long for the germs to get into the nerves and brain. Once that happens, though, the human being is sure to die an agonizing death.

Pasteur did his best to study the disease. He and his assistants trapped every mad dog they heard about and could reach in time. They tied it down and collected the froth from their mouths. (This was very dangerous work.) They injected the froth into rabbits to see what would happen.

The rabbits got the disease but, of course, it took a long time. Then Pasteur tried injecting the froth directly into the rabbit's brain instead of into the blood. The rabbit then got the disease quickly and work could proceed much faster.

Once enough sick rabbits were collected, what could be done? Could Pasteur attenuate the germ as he did the anthrax bacterium? He tried. The germs in the sick rabbits were in the brain and spinal cord. He cut out the spinal cord and heated it gently. Every day he cut off a piece and continued heating the rest.

In this way, he ended with a series of pieces that had been heated for various lengths of time. He soaked each piece in fluid and then injected the fluid into the brains of healthy rabbits. He found that the longer he had heated the piece the milder the disease it caused. A piece that had been heated for two weeks would not give the disease at all.

But would it make an animal immune? Pasteur injected some of his attenuated rabies germ into a healthy dog. Nothing happened. Then he put the dog in a cage with another dog that had rabies. The sick dog promptly began to fight and the healthy dog was bitten. After a while it was rescued and the bites healed. The dog did *not* get rabies.

How could one try it on a human being? You can not deliberately take the chance of giving a human being rabies. But then, on July 4, 1885, a nine-year-old boy named Joseph Meister was badly bitten by a mad dog, and he was rushed to Pasteur as quickly as possible.

Pasteur know that once the disease reached the nerves and brain young Joseph would die. Joseph had nothing to lose if Pasteur experimented, and it had to be done quickly. Pasteur injected some of his

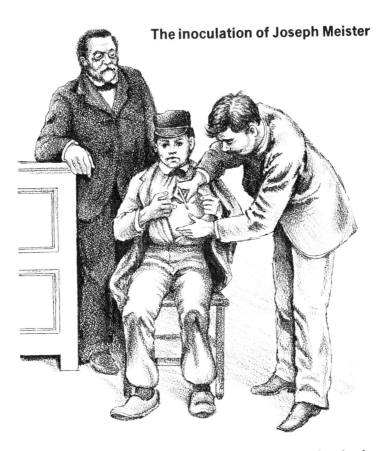

The inoculation of Joseph Meister

most weakened germs to begin helping the body build defenses. He waited a day and injected some less weakened germs. Each day he kept giving Meister stronger germs as his body's defenses developed, until after eleven days Joseph was getting the germs at full strength. He never got rabies!

It was still another triumph for Louis Pasteur, and yet there was one catch. In all his work with rabies,

Pasteur could never find a bacterium, or a germ of any kind, that seemed to cause the disease.

Could it be that the germ theory of disease was wrong? No, Pasteur did not believe that for a moment. Rabies was catching. It could be transferred from one organism to another. *Something* had to be doing the transferring. If nothing could be seen, then maybe it was because the germ was too small to see in a microscope.

This seemed to be true for other diseases, also. No one could find the germ for smallpox, for instance, or the germ for chickenpox, or the germ for influenza, or the germ for the common cold. They were all too small to see.

This was also true for certain diseases that affected organisms other than human beings. Tobacco plants, for instance, suffered from a disease that made their leaves wither. When infected, the leaves would look mottled, as though a mosaic pattern had been drawn

Microscope used by Pasteur

on them. The disease was therefore called "tobacco mosaic disease."

A Russian scientist, Dmitri Ivanovski (ee-VAHN-ov-skee), looked for the germ and could not find it. The juice of mashed leaves from sick plants would cause healthy plants to get the disease, but there was no germ in the juice that he could see.

It occurred to Ivanovski to try to filter the juice. If he could force the juice through something that had tiny holes in it—holes too small to be seen in a microscope—it might stop the very small germs. The liquid would pass through the holes without the germs and would not cause the disease.

Ivanovski used special porcelain filters with particularly tiny holes. In 1892, he forced the juice from sick tobacco leaves through the filters. Even the smallest germ would surely be stopped by it.

But it was not. The fluid that came through would still cause tobacco mosaic disease if placed on the leaves of a healthy plant. Ivanovski had to face the fact that the germs, whatever they were, were small enough to go through even the tiny holes in the porcelain filter. He could not believe that any germs could be *that* small and he just stopped experimenting in that direction.

In 1898, a Dutch botanist, Martinus Willem Beijerinck (BY-er-ink), also tried the very same experiment. He, too, passed the juice of mashed tobacco leaves that had the disease through a porcelain filter. He, too, found that the juice that came through could still infect healthy plants.

59

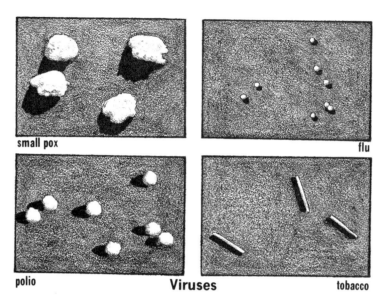

small pox

flu

polio

Viruses

tobacco

He was ready, however, to accept the fact that the germs that caused tobacco mosaic disease were small enough to go through the filter. In fact, he thought the germs might be hardly any bigger than the smallest bits (called "molecules") of water, so that they would go through anything water molecules might go through.

A Latin word for a poisonous juice from plants is "virus." It seemed to Beijerinck that the juice from diseased tobacco leaves was poisonous to healthy tobacco plants, so he called it a virus. The name came to be used for the very tiny germs in the juice.

But how tiny were those viruses? Were they really no larger than water molecules? For a long time, no one could tell.

Then, in 1931, a British scientist, William Joseph

Elford, took up the problem. Why not, he thought, make use of holes still smaller than those in the porcelain filters?

He used collodion instead. Collodion was a thin, transparent membrane, something like cellophane, and it had tiny holes in it. Those holes could be made of different sizes, depending on the exact way in which the collodion was prepared. The holes could be made tinier and tinier and tinier.

Elford forced virus juice through collodion that had holes only about a hundredth as wide as the average bacterium. When that collodion was used, the water was forced through but the virus stayed behind. What came through could not cause disease.

That meant that virus particles might be far smaller than bacteria but were still far larger than water molecules.

Later in the 1930s, special microscopes were invented that made use of beams of tiny particles called "electrons" instead of light. These "electron microscopes" could show things far smaller than anything that could be seen through ordinary microscopes. With the electron microscope, scientists could see viruses at last.

The tobacco mosaic disease virus turned out to be a tiny rod less than half as long as an average bacterium and very skinny, indeed. About 7,000 of these viruses could be fitted inside a single bacterium.

Other viruses were even smaller. The virus that causes yellow fever is so small that 40,000 of them would fit inside an average bacterium.

Even though viruses were too small to be seen without special equipment, they could be guarded against. The first disease to be conquered, smallpox, was caused by a virus after all.

As a result of all the work done by scientists in the last century and a quarter, men are much healthier and live much longer than they used to. Before Pasteur's time, the average European or American lived perhaps forty years. Nowadays, the average lifetime is about seventy years.

Every one of us has, on the average, some thirty extra years of life because of the work of Pasteur and those who followed him.

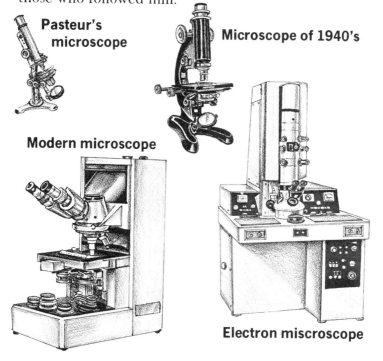

Pasteur's microscope

Microscope of 1940's

Modern microscope

Electron miscroscope

INDEX

Agar-agar, 49-50
Algae, 18
Anthrax, 46-49
Antitoxin, 51
Arsphenamine, 52
Attenuated bacteria, 47-49

Bacteria, 14-16
  attenuated, 47-49
  growing, 49-50
  kinds of, 16-17
  size of, 18
Bacteriology, 18
Behring, Emil Adolf von, 51
Beijerinck, Martinus Willem, 59-60
Black Death, 31

Cohn, Ferdinand Julius, 18-19
Collodion, 61
Cowpox, 33-34

Diphtheria, 51-52
Disease, 31ff.
  immunity from, 32
  microorganisms and, 43-55
  viruses and, 60-62

Ehrlich, Paul, 51
Electron microscopes, 61-62
Elford, William Joseph, 61

Flies, 22-23

Germs, 11, 17
  disease and, 43-55
  very small, 59-62
Germ theory of disease, 43

Immunity, 32, 51
Inoculation, 33
Ivanovski, Dmitri, 59

Jenner, Edward, 33-35

Koch, Robert, 46, 49-50

Leeuwenhoek, Anton van, 12-17
Lenses, 11
  light and, 17
Light, 17
Lister, Joseph, 44-45
Lister, Joseph Jackson, 17

Mad dogs, 54-56
Maggots, 21-24
Meister, Joseph, 56-57
Microorganisms, 14
  disease and, 43-53
  origin of, 24-29
  useful, 44
  wine and, 37-39
Microscopes, 12-18, 62

Muller, Otto Friedrich, 17

Needham, John Turberville, 24

Parasite, 42
Pasteur, Louis, 26
    germ theory of disease and, 41-
        49
    pasteurization and, 37-39
    rabies and, 55-58
    spontaneous generation and,
        26-29
Pasteurization, 38-39
Protozoa, 15

Rabies, 55-57
Redi, Francesco, 22-23

Seeds, 11
Semmelweiss, Ignaz Philipp, 34-
    37

Silkworms, 41-43
Smallpox, 32-34
Spallanzani, Lazzaro, 25
Spontaneous generation, 21-29
    disproof of, 26-29
    pasteurization and, 39
Spore, 46

Tobacco mosaic disease, 58-60
Toxin, 51

Vaccination, 34
Viruses, 60-62
    size of, 61-62

Washing, 37, 44-45

Yeast, 37-38